Disneyland Recipes

Colorful Recipes to Brighten Your Day

BY: DAN BABEL

COOK WITH LOVE

License notes

No part of this publication or its contents may be copied, printed, published, or distributed by any means without the express permission of the author. This book is bound by copyright law, and the author reserves all rights to its publication. While the author has done the required research to ensure that all contents are accurate enough to inform and instruct, the reader is responsible for its content consumption. The author shall not be held accountable to anyone for damages resulting from the text being misinterpreted.

Table of Contents

Introduction

Disneyland recipes can help you by bringing your childhood memories back to you. Individuals with sweet tooth surely don't want to miss the magical recipes.

The recipes are quite easy to prepare and taste awesome.

Once you try them; I guaranty that you would fall in love with them.

From drinks to meals, this book has varieties of Disneyland recipes such as Mint Julep, Strawberry Basil Mint Lemonade, Delicious Hot Chocolate, Delicious Churros, Beauty and the Beast, Disney's Ratatouille, Barbeque Spicy Beef Skewers, Rice Cereal Treats, Lobster Nachos, Mac Cheese Hot Dogs, and many more.

If you haven't tried the Disneyland recipes yet, then this e-book is designed for you in particular. Just download the e-book, turn over the pages, and fall in love with the recipes.

Drinks

Mint Julep

Prep Time: 5 minutes

Cooking Time: 10 minutes

Servings: 10 people

Mint Julep tastes more like "Minty Lemonade" and is a perfect drink for a hot summer day. Enjoy this drink with a little bit of lime, lemon, and mint flavors.

Ingredients

- 1 cup crème de menthe syrup
- 3 cups sugar
- 1/3 cup each of lemonade concentrate limeade concentrate, frozen
- 8 cups water
- Few drops of food coloring, preferably green, optional

For Garnish:

- Fresh mint sprigs
- Lemon wedges
- Maraschino cherries

Directions

Over moderate heat in a large sauce pan, bring the mixture of sugar water to a boil, stirring every now and then.

Let cool for a couple of minutes. Then, pour the mixture into a pitcher, preferably large-sized.

Add in the frozen lemonade limeade concentrates and crème de menthe syrup. Then, add a small amount of green food coloring and give it a good stir until mixed well.

Refrigerate for an hour, until cooled.

Fill a glass with ice. Pour the prepared mixture into it. Serve immediately; garnished with cherries, lemon wedges, and fresh mint sprigs. Enjoy.

Nutritional Value: *kcal: 351, Fat: 1 g, Fiber: 1 g, Protein: 1 g*

Disneyland Dole Whip Float

Prep Time: 1 hour 10 minutes

Cooking Time: 10 minutes

Servings: 6 people

A refreshing and tasty drink to enjoy on a hot sunny day! Rather than filling the glasses with additional pineapple juice, feel free to pour some plain fizzy soda.

Ingredients

- 10 ounces coconut milk
- 4 cups chunks of pineapple, frozen
- 34 ounces (24 plus 10 ounces) pineapple juice
- ½ cup sugar

Directions

Combine all of the ingredients (except 24 ounce of pineapple juice) together in a blender; blend on high power until completely smooth.

Transfer to a freezer bag, preferably gallon-sized; freeze for an hour.

Snip one corner of the bag pipe into individual glasses.

Fill the glasses with some leftover pineapple juice.

Immediately serve garnished with your favorite toppings such as Maraschino cherries, pineapple slices and/or some lemon grass. Enjoy.

Nutritional Value: kcal: 337, Fat: 10 g, Fiber: 2 g, Protein: 2 g

Galaxy's Edge Blue Milk

Prep Time: 5 minutes

Cooking Time: 5 minutes

Servings: 2 people

This is one of the most famous Disneyland drinks, and your kids would surely love the taste. You can even use hints of fruit flavors such as lime, watermelon, passion fruit, and pineapple. Absolutely delicious!

Ingredients

- Blue food coloring, as required
- ¼ teaspoon vanilla extract
- 1 tablespoon fruit punch powder, blue color
- 1 cup ice cubes
- 2 cups whole milk

Directions

In a blender, combine milk with ice, vanilla and fruit punch powder. Cover blend on high power until completely smooth, for a minute or two.

Add a few drops of food coloring; give it a good stir until you get your desired level of color.

Pour the mixture into individual glasses; serve immediately enjoy.

Nutritional Value: kcal: 159, Fat: 8 g, Fiber: 0 g, Protein: 7.7 g

Rose Gold Margarita

Prep Time: 10 minutes

Cooking Time: 10 minutes

Servings: 1 person

Rose gold margarita is a very famous drink in the Magic Kingdom. You can prepare this lovely drink anytime you want and enjoy. Garnish your drink with a few lemon or lime slices.

Ingredients

- 2 ounces Tequila
- 4 ounces Tres Agaves Margarita Mix
- 2 tablespoons guava juice
- 1 tablespoon key lime juice
- 2 tablespoons mango juice
- ½ ounce Grenadine
- 2 tablespoons ginger syrup
- 1 ounce triple sec

Directions

Fill a cocktail shaker with ice. Add all of the ingredients together into it; shake well

Pour the prepared mixture over some ice in a salted rimmed glass. Enjoy.

Nutritional Value: kcal: 941, Fat: 0 g, Fiber: 1 g, Protein: 0 g

Strawberry Basil Mint Lemonade

Prep Time: 5 minutes

Cooking Time: 5 minutes

Servings: 3 people

It's a perfect drink for garden parties. For a fun effect, ensure that 3D Mickey stickers adhere to the paper straws. Feel free to garnish your drink with fresh mint leaves and place some whole strawberries on the side. Enjoy.

Ingredients

- 2 cups strawberries, hulled cut lengthwise into half
- 6 fresh basil leaves
- 1 cup granulated sugar
- 3 cups Meyer lemon juice, freshly squeezed
- 6 cups cold water
- 8 mint leaves

Optional Ingredients:

- Dimensional stickers
- Straws

Directions

Combine sugar with lemon juice in a large pitcher; mix until the sugar has completely dissolved.

Puree the strawberries with basil and mint in a blender until the mixture is completely smooth and then, pour the mixture into the pitcher with sugar-lemon mixture.

Add cold water; give it a good stir until mixed well. Serve over ice and enjoy.

Nutritional Value: kcal: 410, Fat: 1.2 g, Fiber: 10 g, Protein: 4.2 g

Blue Glowtini

Prep Time: 5 minutes

Cooking Time: 5 minutes

Servings: 1 person

I often try this refreshing drink on a hot sunny day, but you can try it anytime you want. If you haven't tried the drink, before then, I strongly recommend you prepare it for you. Certainly, you would fall in love with the taste.

Ingredients

- 1 shot Sweet Sour mix
- 1 shot Skyy Citrus Vodka
- ½ shot peach schnapps
- ½ shot Blue Curacao
- 1 shot pineapple juice

Directions

Fill a shaker with ice and then, combine all of the ingredients in it; shake well.

Then, coat the rim of your martini glass with some sugar and pour the mixture into it. Just before serving; add a blue glow cube. Enjoy.

Nutritional Value: kcal: 200, Fat: 0.2 g, Fiber: 0.1 g, Protein: 0.2 g

Violet Lemonade

Prep Time: 5 minutes

Cooking Time: 5 minutes

Servings: 6 people

You would fall in love with this refreshing lemonade recipe. You don't need to wait for any special occasion; just prepare it anytime you want and enjoy it.

Ingredients

- ½ cup Monin violet syrup
- 8 ounces lemonade concentrate, frozen
- ½ cup lemon juice, fresh
- 2 cups water

Directions

In your blender, blend all of the ingredients together for 30 or more seconds on high power.

Pour the prepared mixture into your large glass. Serve immediately enjoy.

Nutritional Value: kcal: 150, Fat: 0.1 g, Fiber: 2 g, Protein: 0.8 g

Delicious Home Made Horchata

Prep Time: 5 minutes

Cooking Time: 5 minutes

Servings: 1 person

Horchata is one of my favorite holiday beverage recipes. The Mexican cinnamon galleta and cinnamon makes this recipe a hit.

Ingredients

For Horchata:

- ¾ teaspoon vanilla syrup
- ¾ cup condensed milk
- ¼ cup water
- ¾ cup whole milk

For Rice Base

- 2 cups water, preferably filtered
- 1 cup jasmine rice
- 2 cinnamon sticks

For Garnish:

Whipped cream

1 Mexican cinnamon galleta (cookie); cut in half

A pinch of ground cinnamon

Directions

For Rice Base:

Combine jasmine rice with cinnamon sticks water in a large container cover with a lid.

Let sit and ensure rice and cinnamon sticks are softened, for overnight in a refrigerator.

Blend strain well using cheesecloth; set aside until ready to use.

For Horchata:

Combine condensed milk with whole milk in a container, preferably large-sized then, stir into the rice base. Next, stir in the vanilla syrup.

Fill a serving cup with ice and then, pour the prepared Horchata over the ice.

Garnish with a dollop of whipped cream followed by a sprinkle of cinnamon on top.

Create the Mickey ears by placing the Mexican cinnamon galleta over the whipped cream.

Nutritional Value: kcal: 250, Fat: 7.6 g, Fiber: 1.4 g, Protein: 7 g

Frozen Cherry Limeade

Prep Time: 5 minutes

Cooking Time: 5 minutes

Servings: 1 person

Just serve this drink in a sugar coated rimmed glass topped with a fresh cherry and garnished with a lime or lemon wedge. Enjoy.

Ingredients

- 3 ounces non-alcoholic, concentrate margarita mix, frozen
- ¾ ounce grenadine
- 1 ½ ounces Bacardi Torched Cherry Rum

Directions

Pour rum followed by margarita concentrate and grenadine with a cup of ice in a blender.

Blend on high power until completely smooth, for a minute.

Pour into a large glass. Serve chilled and enjoy.

Nutritional Value: kcal: 393, Fat: 0 g, Fiber: 2 g, Protein: 1 g

Delicious Hot Chocolate

Prep Time: 5 minutes

Cooking Time: 10 minutes

Servings: 4 people

This drink is very chocolatey and creamy. You would enjoy every sip. Just serve this recipe on a cold winter day and enjoy it. You can even use cinnamon for dusting.

Ingredients

- 1 cup heavy cream
- 3 cups milk
- 1/8 teaspoon vanilla extract
- 14 ounces condensed milk
- ground cinnamon
- ½ cup grated milk chocolate
- whipped cream
- ½ cup cocoa powder

Directions

First, over medium heat in a large saucepan, combine heavy cream with milk; bring the mixture to a simmer but ensure that you don't bring it to a boil.

Next, combine the grated chocolate with cocoa powder, and approximately ½ cup of heated milk in a small-sized mixing bowl; give the ingredients a good stir until completely smooth. Slowly add this mixture to the saucepan; vigorously whisking the **Ingredients** until completely well.

Then, add in the condensed milk followed by vanilla extract; give the ingredients a good stir until combined well. Let simmer for a couple of minutes.

Ladle the prepared mixture into individual serving cups. Immediately, serve topped with some whipped cream and dusted lightly with the cocoa powder. Enjoy.

Nutritional Value: kcal: 350, Fat: 35 g, Fiber: 4 g, Protein: 19 g

Recipes

Monte Cristo

Prep Time: 20 minutes

Cooking Time: 50 minutes

Servings: 4 people

One of the most delicious recipes that I have ever prepared! This recipe tastes so good that you wouldn't be able to control yourself to make it again. You can try the Monte Cristo recipe for lunch or dinner. You can use any of your favorite grapes for it.

Ingredients

- Vegetable or canola oil

For Batter

- 1 tablespoon baking powder
- 1 ½ cups all-purpose flour
- 1 organic egg, large
- 1 1/3 cups water
- ¼ teaspoon kosher salt

For Sandwiches

- 4 slices Swiss cheese
- 4 slices white bread
- 2 tablespoons sugar, powdered
- 4 slices each of turkey lunch meat ham lunch meat

Directions

Fill a saucepan, preferably medium-sized, approximately ¼ full of the cooking oil and heat until hot, over moderate heat.

For Batter: Stir the flour with baking powder salt in a large-sized mixing bowl until mixed well and then, stir in the egg and water; continue to mix the ingredients until combined well.

For Sandwiches: Layer a slice of Swiss cheese on the bottom slices of bread and then, add 2 slices of each of ham turkey followed by one more slice of the Swiss Cheese. Close with top with a slice of bread cut into fourths; don't forget to insert a toothpick in each prepared slice of sandwich.

Next, coat the sandwich triangle with the prepared batter, preferably on all sides. Don't dip them; simply use a spoon to coat. Work in batches place one of the prepared sandwiches into the hot oil. Cook for a minute or two, until turn golden brown on each side. Remove onto a plate lined with paper towel. Continue the steps mentioned above for the leftover sandwiches.

Cut the warm sandwiches in half and then, dust with the powdered sugar. Arrange them onto a large-sized serving plate with a few strawberries, grapes some blackberry jam on side for dipping. Serve warm enjoy.

Nutritional Value: kcal: 226, Fat: 7 g, Fiber: 1 g, Protein: 11 g

Mickey Mouse Cinnamon Rolls

Prep Time: 10 minutes

Cooking Time: 20 minutes

Servings: 4 people

Enjoy the magic of Disneyland at home. Just serve these delicious breakfast cinnamon rolls for breakfast with a glass full of milk enjoy the taste.

Ingredients

- ¼ cup softened butter
- 2 cans crescent roll dough sheets, refrigerated
- ½ cup brown sugar
- 1 teaspoon vanilla extract
- 2 teaspoons cinnamon
- 1 ½ cups sugar, powdered
- 4 ounces cream cheese, softened
- 1 to 2 tablespoons milk

Directions

Sprinkle the work space with some flour.

Next, roll the refrigerated crescent roll dough out on the prepared surface.

Spread half of butter on each dough rectangle and then, sprinkle with half of brown sugar.

Next, top the rectangles with 1 teaspoon of cinnamon and then, using a pizza cutter; cut each into eight strips.

Now, for the Mickey Mouse head; simply connect two strips of the dough roll up.

For ear, roll up one strip of cinnamon and cover the dough.

Place the Mickey ear and head on a baking sheet lined with parchment; pressing the dough to create a Mickey Mouse

Then, bake for 17 to 20 minutes, at 375 F.

For Cream Cheese Glaze: Add the softened cream cheese into a large-sized mixing bowl and beat using a hand mixer.

Lastly, add powdered sugar and vanilla extract to the beaten cream cheese and mix until completely smooth. If you are actually looking for a thinner consistency; simply add the milk. Drizzle the baked cinnamon rolls with the prepared glaze. Serve immediately enjoy

Nutritional Value: kcal: 588, Fat: 21 g, Fiber: 1 g, Protein: 2.1 g

Delicious Churros

Prep Time: 10 minutes

Cooking Time: 30 minutes

Servings: 16 people

My family just loves these homemade, delicious, cinnamon-sugar coated churros. You can surprise your family with them. This recipe is basically from Mexico; however, it's very famous in Disneyland too.

Ingredients

For Churros:

- 3 organic egg, large
- 1 ¼ cups all purpose flour
- ½ cup butter; cut into small pieces
- 1 ½ cups vegetable oil for frying
- ½ teaspoon vanilla
- 1 cup water
- ¼ teaspoon each of cinnamon salt

For Topping:

- 1 teaspoon cinnamon, divided
- ½ cup sugar

Directions

First, over medium heat in a large, heavy bottomed pot; heat approximately 1 ½" of oil until hot. Next, for topping; whisk the sugar with cinnamon in a shallow dish.

Meanwhile, over moderate heat in a small saucepan; bring water with ¼ teaspoon cinnamon, butter, and salt to a rolling boil. Once done; decrease the heat to low.

Immediately add flour; give it a good stir and form a ball then, remove from the pan from heat. Set aside and let cool for a couple of minutes.

Slowly add in the eggs; stir well after each addition until combined well; set aside until ready to use.

Next, add a star tip, preferably large to a piping bag; spoon the dough into the prepared piping bag. Pipe the dough carefully over the oil cut at 1-3" long. Repeat until the pan is occupied by the churros (ensure that there is still some space in the pan). Fry for 3 minutes per side approximately until turn golden brown.

Once done; using a large slotted spoon, carefully remove the fried churros from oil. Then, arrange them on a plate lined with paper towel.

While the churros are still warm, immediately roll them into the sugar-cinnamon mixture. Serve warm enjoy.

Nutritional Value: kcal: 140, Fat: 8 g, Fiber: 1 g, Protein: 2 g

Beauty and the Beast

Prep Time: 10 minutes

Cooking Time: 20 minutes

Servings: 8 people

Certainly, you would fall in love with this delicious breakfast recipe. The quick breakfast recipe would keep you satisfied till next meal.

Ingredients

- 3 tablespoons instant chocolate pudding mix
- 1 container whipped topping (8 ounces), thawed
- 15 chocolate cookie sandwiches
- 1 (3.4 ounces) package instant vanilla pudding mix
- 12 scalloped sugar cookies
- 1 ½ cups whole milk, cold
- Edible sugar pearls

Directions

Whisk milk with instant vanilla pudding mix in a large-sized mixing bowl until slightly thickened and smooth, for a couple of minutes. Refrigerate until firm, for an hour or two.

Next, in a food processor; pulse the chocolate sandwich cookies until pureed and then, fold into the pudding mix; give the ingredients a good stir until mixed well.

Add in the instant chocolate pudding whipped topping; give the ingredients a stir again until mixed well.

Place in a refrigerator let chill for an hour.

Spoon the grey stuff into piping bag attached with your favorite tip. Pipe the grey stuff over the cookies and then, top with the sugar pearls. Serve and enjoy.

Nutritional Value: kcal: 380, Fat: 19 g, Fiber: 0.1 g, Protein: 4.4 g

Banana Bread

Prep Time: 10 minutes

Cooking Time: 1 hour 10 minutes

Servings: 2 loaves

Absolutely delicious and mouth-watering! For this recipe, you can use frozen ripe bananas and add some nuts as well.

Ingredients

- 2 cups ripe bananas, preferably mashed
- 1 cup butter
- 2 teaspoons baking soda
- 3 cups flour
- 2 organic eggs, large
- ¼ teaspoon vanilla extract
- 2 cups sugar
- 2 teaspoons water
- ½ teaspoon salt

Directions

First, preheat your oven to 350 F.

Second, sift flour with baking soda salt in a large-sized mixing bowl; set aside until ready to use.

Combine the sugar with melted butter until blended well.

Slowly add in the eggs; don't forget to mix the ingredients well after each addition.

Next, add water followed by vanilla and bananas; mix well.

Fold in the flour mixture until incorporated well.

Coat two loaf pans lightly with butter and then, evenly divide the prepared batter between them.

Lastly, bake in the oven until a toothpick comes out clean and middle of your loaf is firm, for an hour.

Nutritional Value: kcal: 410, Fat: 17 g, Fiber: 1.7 g, Protein: 4.8 g

Disneyland Gingerbread

Prep Time: 25 minutes

Cooking Time: 40 minutes

Servings: 12 people

This delicious gingerbread recipe is perfect for any occasion. I served mine with a few MM and a glass full of milk. Quite easy to prepare and taste great! Icing is optional, but it would enhance the taste.

Ingredients

For Gingerbread:

- ½ cup brown sugar
- ¼ cup butter, unsalted
- ½ teaspoon ground cloves
- 3 ½ cups all purpose flour
- ¼ teaspoon ground cardamom
- 1 teaspoon baking soda
- ½ cup "fancy" dark molasses
- 3 teaspoons ground ginger
- ½ cup water
- 1 teaspoon ground cinnamon
- ½ teaspoon salt

For Icing:

- 3 ½ cups sugar, powdered
- 2 egg whites
- ⅛ teaspoon cream of tartar

Directions

For Gingerbread:

Cream the butter with brown sugar in a large-sized mixing bowl.

Add in the dark molasses; continue to mix the ingredients until blended well.

Next, sift the dry ingredients together, work in batches add to the prepared butter mixture alternating with the water. Ensure that you blend the ingredients well.

Using a plastic wrap; cover the dough let chill in a refrigerator for an hour.

Lightly coat the cookie sheets with butter or line them with the parchment paper and then, preheat your oven to 350 F.

Next, roll the dough out on your floured surface using a floured rolling pin, approximately 1/8 to ¼" thick. Feel free to use more of flour, if required.

Cut into standard gingerbread man shapes

Bake for 7 to 10 minutes and then, let it completely cool on the wire racks.

For Icing:

In a chilled large-sized mixing bowl; add cream of tartar with egg whites. Beat the ingredients using an electric mixer until white peaks form, at high speed. Decrease the speed slowly add in the sifted powdered sugar. Continue whipping the ingredients until you get smooth, spreadable like consistency.

Spoon the prepared frosting into plastic baggies with a corner cut off or cake decorating bags; decorate the cookies.

Nutritional Value: kcal: 467, Fat: 4 g, Fiber: 1.2 g, Protein: 4.6 g

Chocolate Peanut Butter Sandwiches

Prep Time: 15 minutes

Cooking Time: 1 hour 15 minutes

Servings: 9 people

This recipe looks very simple, but it tastes delicious and really easy to prepare. I often prepare the recipe for my loved ones, and they just love it. Feel free to store any leftovers in your refrigerator.

Ingredients

- 4 tablespoons softened unsalted butter
- ¾ cup creamy peanut butter
- 1 ½ to 2 cups sugar, powdered
- 2 cups chocolate chips
- 3 tablespoons shortening
- 10 to 12 graham crackers
- ¼ teaspoon salt

Directions

Line a standard-sized baking dish, preferably 9x9" with parchment paper or aluminum foil and then, generously coat it with the nonstick spray; set aside until ready to use.

Next, beat the butter with peanut butter, 1 ½ cups of powdered sugar, and salt using an electric mixer in a large-sized mixing bowl until smooth creamy. Feel free to add more of powdered sugar if the mixture seems to be little sticky until you simply get your desired level of consistency.

Microwave the shortening and chocolate chips in a separate bowl until melted, in 30 seconds intervals, stirring occasionally.

Next, line the bottom of your prepared baking pan with half of graham crackers, preferably in a single layer. Evenly spread 1/3 of the melted chocolate on top. Add in the peanut butter mixture; evenly spreading.

Top with 1/3 more of the melted chocolate; spreading it evenly and then, with one layer of graham crackers then, the leftover chocolate.

Place in a refrigerator for an hour, until set. Once done, slice into desired bars; serve immediately enjoy.

Nutritional Value: kcal: 530, Fat: 32 g, Fiber: 3.5 g, Protein: 6.4 g

Disney World Apple Pie

Prep Time: 1 hour 10 minutes

Cooking Time: 50 minutes

Servings: 9" pie

If you love eating apples and looking for a recipe with apples, then this recipe is specially meant for you. Once you try the recipe, you would forget about any other apple desserts.

Ingredients

For Pie Crust

- 1 ¾ cups all-purpose flour
- ¼ cup shortening
- 4 teaspoons sugar
- 1/3 cup 2% milk
- 4 tablespoons butter, cut into small pieces
- 1/8 teaspoon coarse salt

For Apples

- 2 teaspoon apple pie spice
- 6 apples, preferably granny smith; peeled sliced
- 1 cup water

For Apple Pie Batter

- ½ cup butter, softened
- 2 organic eggs, large
- 2/3 cup sugar
- 1 ½ cups flour
- ¼ cup heavy cream
- 1 ½ teaspoons baking powder
- 1/8 teaspoon salt

Directions

For Pie Crust:

Combine flour with shortening, butter, salt, and sugar using an electric mixer attached with a paddle in a large-sized mixing bowl. Continue to mix the ingredients until crumbly, at medium speed.

Once done; add milk mix for a minute more, until incorporated well. Using a plastic wrap; cover the dough let rest for 30 minutes in a refrigerator.

Roll to approximately ¼" thickness and place in 9" pie plate; set aside until ready to use.

For Apples:

Fill a large pot with water. Then, bring it to a simmer.

Next, add apples in a steamer basket add to the pot. Let steam for 7 to 10 minutes and then, remove from the water. Set aside at room temperature and let cool then, toss with the apple pie spice.

For Apple Pie Batter:

Cream butter with sugar using a stand mixer attached with a paddle in a medium-sized bowl until light fluffy. Slowly add in the eggs; continue to mix until just incorporated.

Next, combine flour with baking powder salt in a small-sized mixing bowl. Slowly add to the mixer continue to beat until combined well, on medium speed.

Add cream continue to mix until completely smooth; set aside until required.

For Apple Pie:

Preheat your oven to 350 F. Place ½ cup of apple pie batter over the pie crust spread until completely smooth. Top with the steamed apples leftover apple pie batter.

Using an aluminum foil; cover bake for 35 to 40 minutes. Remove the foil bake until turn golden brown, for 20 minutes more.

Let cool to room temperature. Just before serving; top the pie with sliced almonds dust with the confectioners' sugar. Enjoy.

Nutritional Value: kcal: 568, Fat: 27 g, Fiber: 4.9 g, Protein: 7.2 g

Disney's Ratatouille

Prep Time: 50 minutes

Cooking Time: 50 minutes

Servings: 4 people

Indeed, this is one of the quickest and easiest recipes that I have ever prepared. Rather than using the tomato paste, feel free to use a jar of pizza quick sauce enjoy.

Ingredients

- 1 eggplant, small, trimmed sliced very thinly
- ½ onion, chopped
- 1 can tomato paste (6 ounces)
- 1 red bell pepper, cored sliced very thinly
- ¼ cup garlic, minced
- 1 tablespoon olive oil
- ¾ cup water
- 1 yellow squash, trimmed sliced very thinly
- 3 tablespoons mascarpone cheese
- 1 teaspoon thyme leaves, fresh, or to taste
- 3 tablespoons olive oil, or to taste
- 1 yellow bell pepper, cored sliced very thinly
- Ground black pepper salt to taste
- 1 zucchini, trimmed sliced very thinly

Directions

Preheat your oven to 375 F in advance.

Spread the tomato paste into the bottom of a baking dish, preferably 10x10" and then, sprinkle with the garlic and onion; add 1 tablespoon of olive oil water; give the ingredients a good stir until combined well and then, season with black pepper and salt.

Arrange alternating slices of red bell pepper, yellow squash, zucchini, yellow bell pepper eggplant; beginning at the outer edge of your dish; working concentrically towards the middle. For colors, feel free to overlap the slices a little and drizzle with 3 tablespoons of olive oil. Season with black pepper and salt. Sprinkle with the thyme leaves. Using a piece of parchment paper; cover the vegetables.

Bake for 40 to 45 minutes, until vegetables are just roasted tender. Serve with a few dollops of the mascarpone cheese. Enjoy.

Nutritional Value: kcal: 324, Fat: 23 g, Fiber: 7.1 g, Protein: 6.1 g

Disneyland Beignets

Prep Time: 20 minutes

Cooking Time: 45 minutes

Servings: 2 people

If you are actually looking for something healthy and easy to prepare, then you must try this recipe at your home. You can also mix some cinnamon with powdered sugar and sprinkle on top. Serve warm and enjoy.

Ingredients

- ½ teaspoon dry yeast
- 2 tablespoons vegetable shortening
- ¼ cup sugar
- 1 organic egg, large
- ½ cup boiling water
- 4 cups all-purpose flour
- ½ cup heavy cream
- Vegetable oil, as required, for frying
- ¼ cup warm water
- Powdered sugar
- ½ teaspoon salt

Directions

In a small-sized mixing bowl; sprinkle the yeast on top of the warm water; give it a good stir until completely dissolved. Let stand for a couple of minutes.

Next, combine shortening with flour, sugar, egg, heavy cream, boiling water and salt in a large-sized mixing bowl and stir into the prepared yeast mixture. Combine the dough using an electric mixer attached the dough hook until just combined smooth, on medium speed. Let the dough to rest for half an hour.

Roll to approximately ¼" thick cut the beignets into 2x3" pieces. Using a towel; cover let the dough to rise in a warm, draft-free area for 1 to 1 ½ hours, until almost doubled in size.

Next, fill a deep-sided pot approximately 2" with oil heat it over medium heat until hot; lightly pressing the beignets until slightly flattened.

Work in batches and add some of prepared beignets into the hot oil; fry until both sides turn golden brown, turning once.

Using a slotted spoon, gradually remove it from the hot oil with arrange them on paper towels lined with baking sheet.

Just before serving; don't forget to dust the cooked beignets with confectioners' sugar. Enjoy.

Nutritional Value: kcal: 414, Fat: 11 g, Fiber: 1.1 g, Protein: 7 g

Disneyland's Churro Toffee

Prep Time: 10 minutes

Cooking Time: 20 minutes

Servings: 20 people

This recipe tastes amazing and is quite easy to prepare. Feel free to omit the almonds and add any of your favorite nuts.

Ingredients

For Toffee:

- 1 cup butter
- ½ cup almonds
- 1 cup granulated sugar
- ½ teaspoon baking soda
- 2 tablespoons water
- 1/3 cup packed brown sugar

For Topping:

- 12 to 16 ounces white chocolate candy coating
- 1 tablespoon cinnamon
- ½ cup granulated sugar

Directions

Preheat your oven to 350 F in advance.

Spread the almonds evenly over a large-sized baking sheet bake in the preheated oven for 7 to 10 minutes.

Let cool until easy to handle. Then, chop them finely.

Next, like the baking sheet with silpat mat or parchment paper; coat it lightly with the non-stick cooking spray. Spread the chopped almonds in a thin layer over the baking sheet.

Next, over medium-high heat in a large, heavy bottomed pot; heat up the butter until melted. Once done, add in both the sugars with water. Bring the mixture to boil, stirring constantly and continue to heat until a candy thermometer reads 300 F.

Immediately remove it from the heat. Stir in the baking soda. Then, pour the prepared toffee on top of the toasted almonds. Thinly spread the toffee across the prepared baking sheet using a lightly greased spatula.

Then, cut the toffee into squares using a lightly greased knife or once the toffee is completely cool; just break it into small pieces using your hands.

Once the toffee is completely cool, stir the cinnamon with sugar in a medium-sized mixing bowl; set aside. Heat up the white chocolate in a microwave safe bowl and then, coat the toffee first with the white chocolate and then, coat it into the sugar-cinnamon mixture. Let cool until the chocolate is just set. Serve and enjoy.

Nutritional Value: kcal: 264, Fat: 14 g, Fiber: 1 g, Protein: 2 g

Disneyland Fried Pickles

Prep Time: 10 minutes

Cooking Time: 20 minutes

Servings: 12 people

These fried pickles with dipping sauce taste amazing! Once you are frying the pickles, ensure that they don't stick to the bottom of the pan or each other.

Ingredients

For Fried Pickles

- 24 ounces dill pickle spears
- ¼ cup grated parmesan cheese
- 2 cups panko breadcrumbs
- 2 lightly beaten eggs, large
- 1 tablespoon fresh parsley, chopped
- Canola oil, for deep frying

For Dipping Sauce:

- 1 teaspoon each of chives, dried parsley flakes fresh dill, chopped
- ½ teaspoon each of onion powder, garlic powder salt
- 1 cup mayonnaise
- ¼ teaspoon ground black pepper
- 1 cup buttermilk

Directions

For Fried Pickles

Place the pickles on a large plate lined with paper towels to absorb any liquid.

Next, stir the breadcrumbs with cheese parsley in a medium-sized mixing bowl until mixed well.

Beat the eggs in a small bowl.

Dip the dried pickle spears first into the egg mixture and then into the bread-crumb mixture; ensure that the pieces are evenly coated. Set aside until ready to use.

Now, over moderate heat in a large saucepan; heat up the oil (enough to submerge the pickles) until hot.

Work in batches fry the coated pickle spears until golden brown, for 3 to 5 minutes; don't overcook them.

Place the fried pickles on a large plate lined with paper towels for a couple of seconds. Serve warm and enjoy.

For Dipping Sauce

In a medium-sized mixing bowl, combine all the dressing ingredients together until mixed well completely smooth. Store in a refrigerator until required.

Nutritional Value: kcal: 207, Fat: 17 g, Fiber: 1 g, Protein: 4 g

Barbeque Spicy Beef Skewers

Prep Time: 10 minutes

Cooking Time: 30 minutes

Servings: 4 people

Your guests' mouths would fill with water after you present this recipe to them. For more heat, feel free to sprinkle some black pepper and crush red chili flakes on top. Serve hot enjoy.

Ingredients

For Beef:

- 18 pieces Sirloin beef chunks (preferably 1 ounce each)
- 2 parts lemon juice, fresh
- 1 part soy sauce
- 6 bamboo skewers
- 1 part water a few grinds of pepper

For Korean Sauce:

- 1 tablespoon ground black pepper
- 1 tablespoon lemon juice, fresh
- 2 tablespoons of brown sugar
- 1 teaspoon vegetable oil
- 1 teaspoon red pepper flakes, crushed
- 3 tablespoons sesame oil
- 1 tablespoon fresh garlic, crushed
- 1 cup water
- ½ teaspoon ground cayenne
- 1 tablespoon corn starch
- 2/3 cup soy sauce

Directions

For Korean Sauce

Over moderate heat in a large saucepan; heat a teaspoon of vegetable oil until hot.

Once done; add one tablespoon of freshly crushed garlic; sauté lightly and ensure that you don't burn it.

Add in the soy sauce followed by lemon juice, red pepper flakes, black pepper, brown sugar, sesame oil, cayenne water; mix well

Decrease the heat to medium-low. Bring the mixture to a slow boil.

Next, decrease the heat to low and let simmer until slightly reduced.

Now, mix 1 tablespoon cornstarch with ¼ cup water in a measuring cup; mix well and then, add the mixture to the simmering sauce.

Let the mixture to simmer until you get thick sauce like consistency.

Taste feel free to adjust the seasonings, as required. Let sit for a couple of minutes.

For Beef:

Cube the Sirloin into 1" pieces.

Put the pieces into a large Ziplock bag and then, add 2 parts lemon juice followed by 1 part of soy sauce, a few grinds of pepper and 1 part of water. Let marinate for 3 hours in a refrigerator.

Once ready to cook; heat the Korean Sauce until warm. Feel free to add soy sauce or a lemon, and some water; if it's too thick.

Put the marinated meat on skewers grill until medium rare, over medium heat and then, remove the skewers on a large plate.

Once done; generously baste the skewers with the prepared Korean Sauce. Serve hot enjoy.

Nutritional Value: kcal: 350, Fat: 24 g, Fiber: 2.1 g, Protein: 11 g

Disneyland Turkey Legs

Prep Time: 1 day 20 minutes

Cooking Time: 1 hour 20 minutes

Servings: 2 people

You would become a fan of this recipe. For variation, I served mine with some freshly prepared mint chutney with green chili (as a dipping). My family just loved it.

Ingredients

- 2 turkey legs
- 2 teaspoons soy sauce
- 2 teaspoons smoked paprika
- 2 tablespoons dark brown sugar
- 1 tablespoon salt

Directions

Combine the brown sugar with paprika, soy sauce and salt in a large-sized mixing bowl; thoroughly stir the ingredients until mixed well.

Next, add the turkey legs in a gallon-sized freezer bag pour the prepared marinade on top; ensure that the prepared rub coats the turkey legs completely. Store in a fridge for overnight.

The follow day; remove the turkey legs from the marinade; pat them dry set aside at room temperature for half an hour.

Roast the turkey legs for 45 minutes, at 325 F. Once done; remove the legs carefully from the hot oven.

Let rest for 5 to 10 minutes. Serve warm enjoy.

Nutritional Value: kcal: 1020, Fat: 46 g, Fiber: 1 g, Protein: 130 g

Apple Granola Pancakes

Prep Time: 10 minutes

Cooking Time: 10 minutes

Servings: 8 people

A nice way to consume apples! This recipe is so delicious and is packed with essential nutrients as well. The best part about the recipe is that you can freeze this dish for up to 3 months.

Ingredients

For Mix

- 2 slightly whisked eggs, large
- 2 teaspoons baking soda
- 4 teaspoons baking powder
- 2 cups buttermilk
- 4 cups flour, sifted
- 2 tablespoons unsalted butter, melted
- ¼ cup sugar
- 2 teaspoons salt

For Apples

- 2 tablespoons butter
- 1 granny smith apple; peeled sliced
- 2 tablespoons brown sugar
- 1 teaspoon cinnamon
- 2 tablespoons sugar

For Topping

- 1 nature valley granola bar, crushed
- Powdered Sugar
- Maple Syrup

Directions

For Apples

In a large skillet, heat up the butter over medium heat until the butter is melted. Once done; immediately add the apples followed by sugars and cinnamon. Cook the ingredients for a couple of minutes, until soft, stirring occasionally.

For Pancakes

First, combine the entire dry Ingredients together in a large-sized mixing bowl; whisk until combined well.

Second, mix all of the wet Ingredients (except butter) together in a separate bowl.

Combine the dry and wet Ingredients together for a couple of minutes, until streaks of flour remain and then, gently fold in the butter. You would be getting a very thick batter.

Now, lightly coat a pan with nonstick spray and then, heat it over medium heat. Cook the pancakes until bubbles form, for a minute or two; carefully flip cook the other side until just set.

To Serve

Place apples on the pancakes and crumble the granola bars and dust with powdered sugar. Serve with syrup.

Nutritional Value: kcal: 280, Fat: 8 g, Fiber: 5 g, Protein: 10 g

Disney Parks Popcorn

Prep Time: 10 minutes

Cooking Time: 10 minutes

Servings: 4 people

Flavacol seasoning makes this recipe a hit. You can even use your pressure cooker with Orville Redenbacher seeds for the recipe. It tastes similar to the Pop Secret Kernels.

Ingredients

- ¼ cup Pop Secret Kernels or
- 1 tablespoon Pop-n-Lite popping oil or Orville popcorn oil
- 1 teaspoon Flavacol Seasoning

Directions

Turn on your popcorn maker

Next, add in the oil and heat it for half a minute, until warm

Add in the popcorn seeds

Then, cook for 2 to 3 minutes approximately, stirring frequently

Transfer the cooked popcorns to a large-sized serving bowl and then, sprinkle with the popcorn seasoning. Serve and enjoy.

Nutritional Value: kcal: 37, Fat: 3 g, Fiber: 0.1 g, Protein: 0.2 g

Rice Cereal Treats

Prep Time: 20 minutes

Cooking Time: 35 minutes

Servings: 8 people

This dish tastes absolutely delicious, and my family is crazy about it. These rice cereal treats would help you remember all the happiest memories that you have spent at Disney World.

Ingredients

- 4 cups miniature marshmallows
- Chocolate Candy Melts
- 6 cups Rice Krispies cereal
- Sprinkles
- 3 tablespoons softened butter

Directions

First, in a large saucepan, heat the butter over low heat until the butter is melted. Add the marshmallows; give it a good stir until melted completely. Immediately remove it from the heat.

Add the Rice Krispies cereal; give it a good stir until coated well.

Evenly press the mixture into 13x9x2" pan; preferably coated lightly with the cooking spray, using a wax paper or buttered spatula. Let cool.

Cut into desired shapes using a Mickey Mouse cookie cutter.

Next, heat the chocolate in a microwave until melted. Start with a 30 second time then add time in 15 second increments.

Dip the top of your Rice Krispie Treat into the chocolate. Arrange them on a pan with parchment paper or wax paper add the sprinkles.

Serve and enjoy.

Nutritional Value: kcal: 200, Fat: 5 g, Fiber: 0.2 g, Protein: 2 g

Berry Pancake Bread Pudding

Prep Time: 10 minutes

Cooking Time: 10 minutes

Servings: 12 people

When we went to Disneyland, we had to order this recipe. I fell in love with the look and taste, so I had prepared my own version of it. This recipe tastes so great that you would continue eating it throughout the day.

Ingredients

For Custard

- 6 organic eggs, large-sized
- 1 ½ cups sugar
- 2 cups half-and-half
- ½ teaspoon nutmeg
- 1 teaspoon vanilla
- 3 cups heavy cream

For Pancakes:

- A batch of homemade pancakes or frozen pancakes, any of your favorite

For Pound Cake

- 1 family size pound cake, sliced cubed

For Fresh Fruit

- 1 to 2 pints each of fresh raspberries fresh blueberries

For Pastry Cream

- 1 ½ teaspoons vanilla extract
- ¾ cup sugar
- 6 egg yolks, large
- ¼ cup all-purpose flour
- 1 ½ cups milk
- ¼ teaspoon salt

For Garnish, Optional

- Powdered sugar

Directions

Whisk the entire custard ingredients (preferably all of it) together in a large mixing bowl; set aside.

Start the process by creating layers for the pancakes; pound the cake crumbles then, blueberries and raspberries; preferably two layers in a large-sized casserole dish, preferably 13x9"

Pour the prepared custard on top of the formed layers, carefully mashing it down and ensure that it soaks the top layers; ensure that you don't squish the berries

Bake for 1 to 1 ½ hours, until the custard is just set, at 350 F. In the meantime, prepare the pastry cream. Combine sugar with flour, milk and salt over medium heat in a 2 quart saucepan. Then, whisk well and continue to cook until the mixture thickens, stirring frequently.

Beat the egg yolks using a large fork in a separate mixing bowl, preferably small-sized; beat a small quantity of the milk mixture to the yolks.

Slowly pour the prepared egg mixture into the milk mixture. Continue to stir cook the ingredients until the mixture thickens, over medium to low heat.

Once done; immediately remove it from heat stir in the vanilla extract. Let the cream to chill until required.

Once done, sprinkle with the powdered sugar serve with the pastry cream. Enjoy.

Nutritional Value: kcal: 644, Fat: 34 g, Fiber: 4 g, Protein: 10 g

S'mores French Toasts

Prep Time: 20 minutes

Cooking Time: 20 minutes

Servings: 2 people

Absolutely delicious and mouth-watering! I used chocolate ganache for this recipe, but you can sub it with Nutella.

Ingredients

- 4 large-sized eggs, preferably organic
- ½ cup milk
- Marshmallow fluff
- 4 bread slices
- 1 tablespoon cinnamon
- Chocolate ganache
- 1 tablespoon vanilla
- Graham cracker crumbs

Directions

For Egg Wash: Whisk the eggs with vanilla, milk and cinnamon in a mixing bowl, preferably large-sized. Place the graham crackers in a different bowl, medium-sized.

Dip both slices of bread first into the egg mixture, turning the pieces a couple of times until both sides are coated evenly. Then coat one side of the bread into graham cracker crumbs.

Cook the bread slices over medium heat, flipping once; set aside.

Spread the chocolate ganache on the uncoated side marshmallow fluff on the other.

Press the slices together. Serve immediately; garnished with more of graham cracker crumbs enjoy

Nutritional Value: kcal: 460, Fat: 14 g, Fiber: 4.8 g, Protein: 22 g

Tonga Toast

Prep Time: 10 minutes

Cooking Time: 40 minutes

Servings: 4 people

Absolutely delicious and easy to prepare! If you are actually looking for something nice and crispy for your guests, then you must try this one.

Ingredients

For Tonga Toast

- 1 loaf sourdough bread (12" long, uncut)
- 2 bananas, large-sized peeled
- 1 quart canola oil, for frying

For Batter

- 1 1/3 cups whole milk
- 4 large eggs
- 1 tablespoon granulated sugar
- ¼ teaspoon cinnamon

For Cinnamon-Sugar Mixture

- 2 teaspoons cinnamon
- ¾ cup granulated sugar

Directions

For Cinnamon-Sugar:

Combine cinnamon with sugar using a fork in a mixing bowl until thoroughly blended; set aside until required.

For Batter:

In a medium-sized mixing bowl, whip the eggs until beaten well. Slowly add the milk followed by sugar, and cinnamon; continue to mix the ingredients until combined well; set aside until ready to use.

For Tonga Toast:

Over moderate heat in a deep fryer or a large pot; heat up the oil until hot.

Slice the bread into four 3" thick slices.

Cut each banana crosswise into half and each piece lengthwise.

Next, place a slice of bread flat on the counter tear out just enough from the middle to stuff half a banana into. Repeat this step with the leftover bread slice.

Dip the stuffed bread into the prepared batter; ensure that you cover both sides. Let any excess batter to drip off. Then, carefully place into the hot oil.

Then, cook until turn golden brown for 4 to 5 minutes. After 2 minutes; turn the toast over cook the other side for 2 minutes, if required. Remove drain the excess oil.

Roll the toast into the sugar-cinnamon mixture. Repeat for each toast. Serve and enjoy.

Nutritional Value: kcal: 520, Fat: 8 g, Fiber: 6 g, Protein: 11 g

Pumpkin Spice Waffle

Prep Time: 15 minutes

Cooking Time: 10 minutes

Servings: 8 people

You would even start licking your fingers once you try this recipe at home. You can even add ¼ cup each of coconut flour oat flour for the recipe. Just before serving, feel free to delectably add some butter on top.

Ingredients

- 6 tablespoons melted butter, unsalted
- 1 cup solid-pack pumpkin, canned
- 2 ¼ teaspoons baking powder
- 1 teaspoon baking soda
- 2 ½ cups all-purpose flour
- A pint of buttermilk, vigorously shaken
- 2 teaspoons ground cinnamon
- ⅓ cup light brown sugar, packed
- 4 organic eggs, separated
- 1 teaspoon ground ginger
- ¼ teaspoon ground cloves
- 1 serving cooking spray
- ½ teaspoon salt

Directions

Preheat a waffle iron pre the mentioned directions.

Next, beat the egg whites in a metal or glass bowl until soft peaks form for a minute or two.

Beat the egg yolks with pumpkin, buttermilk butter in a large-sized mixing bowl using a whisk until completely smooth; add flour followed by cinnamon, brown sugar, baking soda, baking powder, ginger, cloves, and salt. Stir the mixture using the whisk until you just get smooth batter like consistency.

Then, fold the egg whites into the batter until just combined.

Prepare the cooking surfaces of waffle iron with the cooking spray. Ladle approximately 2/3 cup of the prepared batter into the hot iron cook for 4 to 5 minutes, until browned.

Nutritional Value: kcal: 327, Fat: 11 g, Fiber: 2 g, Protein: 10 g

Lobster Nachos

Prep Time: 10 minutes

Cooking Time: 4 hours 10 minutes

Servings: 12 people

This recipe is actually one of my favorite recipes. Though the recipe requires some time and some of your efforts, but the end results are delicious. For more heat, feel free to evenly sprinkle some black pepper and chili flakes on top.

Ingredients

For Lobster:

- Juice zest of 1 lime
- 5 medium lobster tails (meat only)
- A pinch of black pepper
- 4 tablespoons butter
- ½ teaspoon coarse salt

For Lobster Cheese Sauce:

- 4 ounces grated Oaxaca cheese
- 1 cup reduced lobster stock
- 3 Polanco chiles, chopped roughly
- 1 shallot, roughly chopped
- 3 garlic cloves, large
- 1 teaspoon canola oil, divided
- 2 ½ tablespoons flour
- 2 cups manufacturing cream
- ¼ stick butter
- 2 cups sharp cheddar cheese, grated

For Lobster Stock:

- 1 carrot, medium, chopped
- Shells from 5 lobster tails, medium-sized
- 1 onion, small, chopped
- 2 garlic cloves, large, quartered
- 1 fresh celery rib, small, chopped
- ½ cup dry white wine
- 1 bay leaf
- ¼ bunch fresh parsley (only stems)
- 8 cups cold water
- 1 teaspoon canola oil
- A pinch of red pepper flakes

For Seasoned Black Beans

- 1 small bunch cilantro chopped
- 1 can black beans (15 ounces)
- ½ teaspoon kosher salt
- 1 teaspoon ground cumin

For Tortilla Chips

- 3 cups canola oil
- 48 corn tortillas (6" each, approximately 4 dozen)
- Salt, as required

For Shredded Cheese:

- ½ pound each of Monterey jack cheese cheddar cheese

For Pico De Gallo

- ½ medium red onion, diced
- 5 Roma tomatoes, diced
- ½ bunch fresh cilantro, chopped (only tops)
- 1 ½ tablespoons lime juice, fresh
- 1 Serrano pepper, remove the seeds, finely minced
- 1 teaspoon salt

For Chipotle Crema:

- 2 garlic cloves, roasted
- 1 ½ tablespoons chipotle in adobo sauce
- 8 ounces sour cream
- A pinch each of ground cumin ground black pepper
- 3 tablespoons cream
- ½ teaspoon salt

For Roasted Garlic:

- 2 garlic cloves, large
- Canola oil (enough to cover)

Directions

For Lobster Stock:

Preheat your oven to 350 F.

Place the lobster shells with celery, carrot, garlic, and onion on a large-sized baking sheet and then, lightly coat with the canola oil.

Bake in the preheated oven until browned lightly, for 30 to 35 minutes.

Once done; remove from the oven using some white wine; deglaze the baking sheet.

Add the ingredients of baking sheet with its liquid to a stockpot, preferably large-sized.

Add water, red pepper flakes, parsley, and bay leaf.

Bring the lobster stock to a boil. Once done, decrease the heat to medium low and continue to cook for 60 to 70 minutes, until stock decreases by half.

Carefully strain the stock; keep a cup aside for the lobster cheese sauce.

For Tortilla Chips:

First, over moderate heat in a large saucepan, preheat the oil until hot.

Meanwhile, cut the tortillas into 6 pieces, preferably pie-shaped.

Next, once the oil is hot, work in batches add a few pieces of tortillas into the hot oil; fry until browned lightly, for 2 to 3 minutes.

Remove the fried chips and season it lightly with some salt.

Continue to cook the tortillas until all are fried salted; set aside until required.

For Seasoned Black Beans:

Rinse the beans in a colander for a couple of times until water runs clear.

Place the rinsed beans into a medium-sized mixing bowl and mix with the leftover ingredients until combined. Then, set aside until ready to use.

For Pico De Gallo:

Combine all of the ingredients (except serrano pepper) together in a medium-sized mixing bowl.

Add half of the Serrano pepper; continue to mix taste; add more of Serrano pepper until desired level of spiciness is achieved; set aside.

For Mixed Cheese:

Grate the Monterey jack and cheddar cheeses in a medium-sized mixing bowl; toss well set aside.

For Roasted Garlic:

1. Remove the tips from garlic cloves.

Add the garlic to small pot add in the canola oil (enough to cover).

Gently poach the garlic until soft and browned lightly, over medium-low heat.

Remove the garlic; set aside for use in chipotle crema (you can reserve the garlic oil in a refrigerator for cooking different dishes).

For Chipotle Crema:

Purée the roasted garlic and chipotle in a food processor.

Add the purée leftover ingredients to a large-sized mixing bowl; thoroughly mix the **Ingredients**.

Pour the crema in a plastic zip bag or squeeze bottle.

Refrigerate until required.

For Lobster Cheese Sauce:

First, preheat your oven to 350 F.

Lightly coat the Polanco peppers with approximately ½ teaspoon of canola oil and then, arrange it on a baking sheet, preferably evenly spaced; roast in the preheated oven for 12 to 15 minutes.

Coat the garlic and shallots lightly with the leftover canola oil and then, add to the baking sheet with Polanco peppers; roast until caramelized, for 20 to 25 more minutes.

Purée the Polanco peppers, shallots, and caramelized garlic in a food processor until completely smooth.

Next, over medium heat in a large pot; heat up the butter until melted.

Add flour to the melted butter and prepare a roux; continue to cook for 4 to 5 minutes, until light golden brown smooth, stirring it frequently.

Add cream; bring the mixture to a boil; continue to stir cook for 10 minutes, stirring constantly.

Add in the Polanco pepper purée and reserved lobster stock; bring it to a simmer, stirring every now and then.

Slowly add in the cheddar and Oaxaca cheeses.

Give the ingredients a good stir until sauce is completely smooth, all of the cheese is melted.

Set aside; hold warm.

For Cooked Lobster:

Ensure that the lobster meat is cleaned veins removed.

Chop the lobster in large pieces, preferably bite-sized.

Next, over medium heat in large sauté pan; heat up the butter until melted.

Add in the pieces of lobster followed by pepper, juice zest of lime, and salt to the hot pan.

Once cooked, immediately remove the pieces lobster using a large slotted spoon. Set aside.

To Serve:

Preheat your broiler to 500 F in advance. Spread the chips on 2 medium or 1 large oven-safe plate.

Layer with the black beans followed by lobster cheese sauce, and mixed jack/cheddar cheese; ensure that you cover the chips completely.

Broil for 2 to 5 minutes, until the cheese is completely melted.

Carefully remove the sheet/plate and then, add in the pico de gallo then, top with the cooked lobster.

Drizzle with the chipotle crema garnish with Serrano peppers (sliced). Serve immediately enjoy.

Nutritional Value: kcal: 470, Fat: 26 g, Fiber: 4 g, Protein: 20 g

Mickey Mouse Chicken Noodle Soup

Prep Time: 10 minutes

Cooking Time: 20 minutes

Servings: 8 people

I never thought of preparing this soup at home but did it for my kids. They just loved the taste and asked for more. For the chicken, feel free to use light or dark meat. Both taste great.

Ingredients

- 14 ounces pasta, preferably Mickey mouse shaped
- 2 teaspoons fresh rosemary, minced
- 1 large yellow onion, diced
- 12 cups chicken stock
- 2 carrots, peeled diced
- 4 sticks celery, diced
- 2 heaping cups chicken; cooked shredded
- 3 garlic cloves, minced
- 1 tablespoon fresh thyme, minced
- 2 tablespoons olive oil
- Pepper salt, to taste

Directions

Over medium heat in a large heavy bottomed pot; heat the olive oil until hot. Once done; add the onion followed by celery and carrots; sauté for 5 to 7 minutes, until softened.

Add garlic, rosemary and thyme; give the ingredients a good stir cook for a minute. Add chicken and chicken stock, bring the mixture to a boil.

Add pasta continue to cook for 6 to 8 more minutes, until soft. Season with pepper and salt to taste; serve hot enjoy.

Nutritional Value: kcal: 430, Fat: 12 g, Fiber: 3 g, Protein: 24 g

Grilled Cheese Tomato Soup

Prep Time: 10 minutes

Cooking Time: 35 minutes

Servings: 4 people

These grilled cheese sandwiches are just amazing. I served this recipe to my family on a cold winter day. I added a cube of butter over the hot soup and sprinkled with a pinch of black pepper.

Ingredients

For Grilled Cheese Sandwiches:

- 2 cups extra sharp cheddar cheese, shredded
- 6 tablespoons softened butter
- 2 cups gruyere cheese, shredded
- 8 slices sourdough bread

For Tomato Basil Soup:

- 1 large can peeled tomatoes in juice (28 ounces; crushed well using your hands)
- 3 tablespoon ghee
- 1 large onion, diced
- 2 ½ tablespoons tomato paste
- ½ to 1 teaspoon black pepper
- 4 garlic cloves, diced
- ¼ teaspoon cayenne, optional
- 4 cups chicken stock
- A large handful of roughly chopped fresh basil leaves
- ¼ cup heavy cream
- 1 tablespoon sea salt

Directions

For Tomato Basil Soup:

Over medium to low heat in a large pot; heat the ghee until melted and then, add the onion; sauté until browned, for 15 to 20 minutes.

Add garlic continue to sauté for a couple of more minutes.

Add in the tomato paste sauté for a minute more.

Mix in the chicken broth, cayenne, pepper, and salt.

Stir in the crushed tomatoes; cover the pot with the lid and bring it to a gentle boil. Once done, decrease the heat to low. In the meantime, prepare the grilled cheese sandwiches. A couple of minutes before you plan to serve the dish, stir in the cream and basil to the hot soup.

For Grilled Cheese Sandwiches:

Place the nonstick pan / griddle on medium low heat.

Generously butter each of the sourdough bread slices, on one side.

Once the pan / griddle is hot; place the slice of bread, butter-side down on it

Add a hefty handful of cheese to each slice top with one more slice of bread, butter side up.

After a couple of minutes, gradually flip the sandwich to brown the other side for 2 more minutes.

Remove from the heat; slice serve with the hot tomato basil soup. Enjoy.

Nutritional Value: kcal: 1347, Fat: 80 g, Fiber: 6 g, Protein: 60 g

Kahua Pulled Pork Sliders

Prep Time: 20 minutes

Cooking Time: 5 hours 30 minutes

Servings: 12 people

It tastes great when served warm with some chili tomato sauce on the side. You must try this recipe for your guests if you really want to surprise them with your cooking skills.

Ingredients

- 5 pounds pork shoulder, preferably boneless
- 2 tablespoons Red Hawaiian sea salt
- 3 tablespoons garlic, minced
- 1 tablespoon ginger, chopped
- 2 tablespoons Liquid Smoke

Directions

First, preheat your oven to 325 F.

Line a large, oven-safe roasting pan with aluminum foil.

Score the meat by making deep cuts approximately 1 to 2" apart.

Next, pour the Liquid Smoke into the deep cuts of the meat

Rub ginger, garlic ½ of sea salt into the deep cuts of meat.

Then, wrap the pork shoulder snugly using aluminum foil; ensure that it covers the meat completely and there are no opened areas or gaps.

Bake for 4 to 5 hours. Once done; remove the meat from oven place in a large-sized serving bowl then, shred with two large forks. Sprinkle the shredded meat with leftover salt serve with the Hawaiian Sweet Rolls. Enjoy.

Nutritional Value*: kcal: 457, Fat: 5.5 g, Fiber: 2.8 g, Protein: 2 g*

Three Cheese Sandwiches

Prep Time: 20 minutes

Cooking Time: 30 minutes

Servings: 4 people

This recipe is one of the latest Disneyland recipes. Feel free to sub the Double Gloucester cheese with shredded cheddar for the cream cheese spread.

Ingredients

- 8 slices provolone
- 8 slices artisan bread
- 8 slices cheddar cheese
- For Garlic Spread:
- 1 ½ teaspoons garlic, minced
- 1 cup mayonnaise
- ½ teaspoon coarse salt
- For Spread:
- ½ cup cream cheese
- 2 tablespoons heavy cream
- ½ cup Double Gloucester cheese
- ¼ teaspoon of coarse salt

Directions

For Spread:

Blend the cream cheese with Double Gloucester, heavy cream salt in a food processor until completely smooth; set the mixture aside until ready to use.

Garlic Spread:

Combine mayonnaise with garlic salt in a small-sized mixing bowl; give the **Ingredients** a good stir for a minute or two approximately until blended well; set the mixture aside.

For Sandwich:

Lay the slices of artisan bread out on a large-sized cutting board or parchment paper.

Place 2 cheddar slices on 4 slices of bread. Place 2 provolone slices on the leftover bread slices.

Evenly spoon the prepared cream cheese spread over the slices with the provolone. Smooth the spread gently on each slice, pressing the provolone side and cheddar side together.

Next, brush the sandwiches with the garlic spread, preferably on both sides. In a large skillet, grill the sandwiches over medium heat until the cheese is completely melted bread turns golden brown, for 2 minutes per side.

Nutritional Value: kcal: 1150, Fat: 90 g, Fiber: 2 g, Protein: 40 g

Mac Cheese Hot Dogs

Prep Time: 10 minutes

Cooking Time: 20 minutes

Servings: 8 people

Do you love hot dogs and looking for their recipes? You must go for this one. These hot dogs are topped with crispy bacon and truffle Mac Cheese.

Ingredients

- 8 ounces American cheese
- 8 ounces macaroni
- 4 ounces half and half
- 8 slices bacon; cooked until crisp
- 8 hot dogs
- ½ teaspoon truffle oil
- 8 hot dog buns

Directions

Prepare the pasta per the directions mentioned on the package.

Heat the American cheese with half and half over moderate heat in a small pot until the sauce is completely smooth creamy texture, stirring occasionally. Add truffle oil into the cheese and macaroni; blend the oil into the cheese sauce.

Once done; pour the pasta into cheese sauce; ensure that you completely coat the pasta with the prepared cheese sauce. Cook the hot dogs until warm. Place the hot dogs into buns then spoon a few tablespoons of the macaroni-cheese over the warmed hot dogs. Add the crumbled bacon over macaroni cheese. Serve immediately enjoy.

Nutritional Value: kcal: 430, Fat: 21 g, Fiber: 1.4 g, Protein: 16 g

Chicken and Sausage Gumbo

Prep Time: 20 minutes

Cooking Time: 1 hour 40 minutes

Servings: 8 people

Once you present this recipe to your guests, they wouldn't be able to control themselves. I served mine with freshly prepared Nan, but you can serve it with anything of your choice.

Ingredients

- 1 pound chicken breasts, boneless, skinless
- ¾ cup vegetable oil
- 1 pound boneless, skinless chicken thighs
- 2 tablespoons extra virgin olive oil
- 1 teaspoon ground black pepper
- 12 ounces andouille sausage, cooked sliced
- 1 cup unbleached, all purpose flour
- ¼ teaspoon cayenne powder
- 1 tablespoon coarse salt
- 2 celery ribs, halved sliced
- 1 bell pepper, diced (½ green ½ red)
- 4 garlic cloves, minced
- ½ yellow onion, diced
- 2 cups okra, fresh or frozen; sliced
- 1 ½ teaspoons gumbo file
- 6 cups chicken broth
- 1 tablespoon Creole or Cajun seasoning
- ¼ teaspoon Tabasco or to taste
- 2 to 3 bay leaves
- Pepper salt to taste

For Garnish:

- Green onion, roughly sliced
- Fresh parsley, roughly chopped

Directions

For Roux: Over medium heat in a medium sized skillet; heat the vegetable oil until hot. Once done; whisk in the flour cook until turn dark brown, for 25 to 30 minutes, whisking every now and then; ensure that you don't burn the roux. Set aside in a warm place until ready to use.

Using a paper towel; pat the chicken breasts and chicken thighs dry then, evenly season on both sides with pepper and salt.

Next, over medium high heat in a large, heavy bottomed pot; add 1 tablespoon of olive oil until it starts shimmering. Once done; work in batches add the chicken sear for a minute or two on each side. You may need to do half at a time to avoid over; ensure that you don't over crowd the pot. Then, remove the chicken pieces to a large plate.

Pour approximately ½ cup of chicken broth into the pot, scrapping up any browned bits from the bottom.

Add the leftover olive oil followed by bell pepper, onion, okra and celery; sauté for 3 to 5 minutes approximately until the onion begins to turn translucent.

Add garlic, Creole or Cajun seasoning, cayenne powder continue to sauté for a minute more.

Stir in the sausage, adding the chicken pieces into the pot again.

Add the roux; give the ingredients a good stir until coated evenly with the mixture.

Pour in approximately 4 ½ cups of chicken broth followed by the Tabasco. Add the bay leaves. Bring the mixture to a boil. Once done; decrease the heat and let simmer then, loosely cover. Continue to cook for half an hour more, stirring every now and then.

Remove the gumbo from heat. Feel free to add more of chicken broth as required until you get your desired consistency. Stir in the gumbo file. Immediately add pepper, salt, and more of Tabasco, as required. Serve; garnished with parsley and green onion.

Nutritional Value*: kcal: 540, Fat: 40 g, Fiber: 2.7 g, Protein: 31 g*

Delicious Fried Chicken

Prep Time: 20 minutes

Cooking Time: 30 minutes

Servings: 6 people

If you are certainly looking for a healthy snack recipe for your loved ones, then you must give this recipe a try. I served mine with some freshly prepared mint chutney.

Ingredients

- 3 cups all-purpose flour
- 2 pounds chicken pieces (preferably thighs, breasts legs)
- 4 large eggs, lightly beaten
- 3 cups buttermilk
- 4 cups vegetable shortening, for frying
- Ground black pepper kosher salt to taste

Directions

First, place the chicken pieces, skin side down in a shallow container pour in the buttermilk. Using a plastic wrap; cover let marinate overnight in a refrigerator.

Second, preheat your oven to 375 F in advance.

Remove the chicken from buttermilk season with pepper salt on both sides.

Then, place the flour and beaten eggs in separate shallow bowls. Dredge the chicken pieces into the flour and then, into the egg finally into the flour again.

Over moderate heat in a 12" sauté pan with deep sides; heat the oil until the oil starts to smoke. Work in batches fry the chicken until the skin turns golden brown for 2 minutes per side. Transfer to a large-sized baking sheet bake the chicken until cooked through, for 12 to 15 minutes.

Nutritional Value: kcal: 310, Fat: 4 g, Fiber: 1.3 g, Protein: 13 g

Grilled Breakfast Burrito

Prep Time: 20 minutes

Cooking Time: 30 minutes

Servings: 4 people

Just start your day with this delicious breakfast burrito. It is packed with essential nutrients and vitamins and would keep you full till your next meal.

Ingredients

- 2 to 4 strips bacon or turkey bacon
- Burrito sized Tortilla
- 2 to 3 organic eggs, large
- A pinch of salt
- 2 to 4 Pork breakfast sausage patties or turkey sausage or sausage links
- Pico de Gallo
- ½ to 1 cup of hash browns

Directions

Prepare your breakfast sausage by heating them; set them aside on a large plate lined with paper towel to drain any grease.

Thoroughly cook the bacon over medium-high heat; ensure that you don't burn them; set them aside with the prepared sausage.

Whisk the eggs in a large-sized mixing bowl, and then add a pinch of salt; cook them scrambled in the bacon grease. Lay your tortilla out on a large plate. Stack the eggs as the base. Add on the pico de gallo followed by the bacon and finally the sausage.

Next, fold in the left right sides first. Ensure the corners are curving in not out. Then, carefully fold in the side closer to you while still holding the left right sides intact. Gradually roll the burrito to close up the rest of the rest of the way. Heat the wrapped burrito on a hot griddle or pan for a couple of minutes per side. Wrap in aluminum foil; serve immediately enjoy.

Nutritional Value*: kcal: 314, Fat: 22 g, Fiber: 1 g, Protein: 12 g*

Conclusion

Thank you again for downloading this e-book.

The book has plenty of Disneyland inspired recipes which can bring some magic and can spice up your life.

You don't need anything else with the recipes mentioned in the e-book since they are doable, easy to prepare not that costly.

What are you still waiting for? If you haven't downloaded this e-book till yet, then do it now and give your loved ones a healthy treat that they deserve.

Author's Afterthoughts

It's incredible to think that I hesitated to publish my book, thinking that it wouldn't get as much as a single attention from anyone. But here we are. You all have bought and accepted this book, and it means more than you can ever imagine. So, here's me asking for one more favor. I would love to know your thoughts on this book. Your feedback will mean a lot to me and help others who are searching for the right book.

Thanks,

Dan Babel

About the Author

From humble beginnings in a little town in Florida to the big stage, Dan Babel had always known that his path included a lot of food. As a child, he was always in the kitchen with his mother and grandmother. Most times, it was to see what he could grab when no one was looking. However, he was also attracted to what he saw as "magic." He wondered how something as white and simple as flour could create the delicious cakes he could never let go of. His curiosity led him from just eating the meals to being a part of the cooking process.

As a natural, Dan realized that it didn't take long for him to learn even the most complex of recipes. It was inevitable that he would head to culinary school just after he completed high school. After his graduation, Dan worked with a team of chefs whose specialty was traditional Asian dishes. Thanks to the skills learned here, he went on to open up his restaurant. It has been close to a decade, and it keeps getting better.

Made in the USA
Las Vegas, NV
03 December 2020